CHARACTERS OF THE TURF

CHARACTERS OF THE TURF

BY

PETER A MASON & NIALL O'LOUGHLIN

Published By Avalon Promotions
Laytown, Co.Meath
Ireland

Copyright © Leonard Kinsella

All rights reserved. No part of this publication may be reproduced,
stored in a retrieval system or transmitted, in any form or by any means,
without the prior permission in writing of the publisher, nor be otherwise
circulated in any form of binding or cover other than that in which it is published
and without a similar condition including this condition being
imposed on the subsequent purchaser.

Contents

Owners

Fr. Sean Breen	10	Dermot Desmond	12
William Durkan	14	Michael Futter	16
John Magnier	18	J. P. McManus	20
Michael O'Leary	22	Lady Chryss O'Reilly	24
Michael Ryan	26		

Trainers

Jim Bolger	30	Michael Halford	32
Jessica Harrington	34	Michael Hourigan	36
Dessie Hughes	38	Noel Meade	40
Arthur Moore	42	Joanna Morgan	44
Michael Morris	46	Willie Mullins	48
Aidan O'Brien	50	Eddie O'Grady	52
John Oxx	54	Kevin Prendergast	56
Christy Roche	58	Tommy Stack	60
Charlie Swan	62	Tom Taaffe	64
Ted Walsh	66	Dermot Weld	68

Jockeys

Nina Carberry	72	Paul Carberry	74
Kieren Fallon	76	Barry Geraghty	78
Michael Kinane	80	Kevin Manning	82
Tony McCoy	84	Declan McDonagh	86
Johnny Murtagh	88	Conor O'Dwyer	90
Pat Smullen	92	Ruby Walsh	94

Bookmakers - Presenters

Justin Carthy	98	Frank Finigan	100
Gearoid Moynihan	102	Gareth O'Brien	104
Hector O'Heochagain	106	Tracy Piggott	108
Paddy Power	110		

INTRODUCTION

Ever since my first visit to Ireland in 1993, to work at the Galway Festival, it has almost been a love affair for me with this great island. I made a point of coming over again later that year to Tralee and, up until the summer of 2005 I had made hundreds of trips across the water. In September of that year I packed my bags and here I am enjoying my racing more than ever.

Gone are the days of me working at the tracks, setting up a marquee in all elements, selling art, limited edition prints, greeting cards etc. After all, I'd had eighteen years of it. But I have to be thankful to all those racecourse managers who allowed me to work at their racecourses, the racegoers who purchased goods from me and the many friends that I have met in over 14 years, of my time spent in Ireland.

But this book is all down to the characters involved in racing whom I've met and come to admire and appreciate and, no doubt there are many, many more who are not featured in this book who possibly think they deserve a mention. To them I apologise.

The owners, trainers, jockeys, bookmakers and presenters featured are real characters of the turf, the like you'd never meet in any other country. Tracy Piggott once explained to me, the people here are honest and straight with you and that this country really took her to heart. Even when she had a lucrative opportunity to return home to England to work for the BBC, she declined. Because she actually feels she is at home. I know what she meant and I have had that feeling for some time now myself and I, like Tracy, would never consider returning to England in the future.

As well as meeting and writing about these characters there is one person who I admire above all others, the lady who captured my heart at the summer festival at Bellewstown more than two years ago. Even when writing this book I have so much to thank her for, like picking me up whenever I was feeling down or, whenever I was getting complacent she would kick "my arse into gear". But Mary has been has been my inspiration and rock and, probably without her I may never have put pen to paper. I suppose I have Kevin Coleman to thank, in a way, for meeting this wonderful lady.

I have to thank all these great horseracing characters who have made it into this book, their individual style, their achievements within the sport and the assistance they gave me in my research.

Niall O'Loughlin, the artist, what can I say about this guy ? He is the most brilliant caricaturist that I've ever met, quiet and unassuming, the ultimate professional. The long hours and dedication he has devoted into completing this book on time is commendable. I must also thank his wife, Helena, for letting him get on with it. And I look forward to working with him again in the very near future.

And to my good friend, Leonard Kinsella, my grateful thanks as he has been very supportive of this venture and without whom, you definitely wouldn't be reading this now.

There will be a donation made by Avalon Promotions from the sales of
"Characters Of The Turf" to the Injured Jockeys Fund.

Enjoy !

NIALL O'LOUGHLIN

Born in Dublin in 1970, Niall graduated from the Senior College Ballyfermot in 1989 and spent the next 10 years working as an animator throughout the world.

Projects he worked on included 'Teenage Ninja Turtles', 'All Dogs Go To Heaven', 'Help I'm A Fish' and 'Give up yer aul sins'.

In 2001, Niall, disillusioned with the way he saw the animation industry was heading took the plunge, and followed his true passion to become a full time caricaturist.

He spent the next 3 years building his business, and in December 2004 became the first caricaturist to have his work showcased on the world's longest running chat show, 'The Late Late Show'.

In 2006, Niall held his first solo exhibition in Dublin, which received massive television and press coverage, and firmly cemented his name as Irelands foremost caricaturist.

Niall currently lives in Dunboyne, Co Meath with his wife Helena and 3 boys Rían, Oran and Illan.

OWNERS

Fr. Sean Breen

Fr. Sean Breen was born in Cavan nearly 71 years ago and gets a great buzz out of not only owning racehorses but, primarily just going to the races. He is quick to point out that he is "a proud Ulsterman and, that is all he has in common with Rev. Ian Paisley".

There was no family involvement with horses whatsoever, father being a teacher and mother "an unpaid housekeeper" but, she was worth her weight in gold as she brought up five boys and two daughters. A neighbour of the family owned ponies and Sean and his brother, Oliver, would learn to ride them on their neighbour's farm.

Later, Oliver qualified to become a dentist and moved to England where he met a lot of fellow professionals who knew a bit about horse racing. On his return home he'd be telling Sean he's been to Sandown, Kempton, Ascot etc.

The family moved from the country down to Dublin in 1956 as father couldn't afford to keep a country home, a townhouse and send the kids to college. Leopardstown racecourse became Breen's first visit to an Irish track and he later moved to Ballymun.
Whenever asked where he was educated, he would say "Ballymun flats - the school of experience".

Being in North Dublin, he got to meet and become friends with the Dreapers, great horsemen of that era. Horses like Brown Lad and Ten Up stirred Breen's passion for the jumping game. However, his first visit to the Cheltenham Festival was to see the great Arkle record the first of his three Gold Cup triumphs and, now over forty years on, Breen recollects only ever missing two subsequent Festivals.

In the mid-seventies he met up with Joanna Morgan and she has been virtually training horses for him ever since. One Won One was a multiple winner including a Group Three race at The Curragh and, another decent horse they've had between them was Portant Fella who, in August 2006, won a two mile novice chase at Roscommon and a seven furlong race at Laytown, within twenty four hours of each other.

One dual purpose horse Breen had was Christiansted, trained by Ferdy Murphy in North Yorkshire, and who managed to rattle up six victories in the UK.

Fr. Breen is a very keen Sunderland soccer supporter ever since he struck up a friendship with chairman and racehorse owner and breeder, Niall Quinn.

Long may he be saying mass at the Galway Races and marking our card
for that first Sunday in August.

FR. SEAN BREEN

DERMOT DESMOND

Dermot Desmond, a proud Cork man, is regarded as one of Ireland's most successful and richest entrepreneurs.

From selling football programmes outside Tolka Park in Drumcondra to being the owner of Celtic Football Club and many other companies beside, has made Desmond a respected figure in the business world and worth in excess of €2 billion.

After leaving school in 1968 Desmond had an early successful career in banking.

He shares his interests in horse racing with business partners and best friends, John Magnier and J.P.McManus, with whom he owns the Sandy Lane Hotel in Barbados with. Desmond also owns Betdaq, the Irish betting exchange and the Sporting Emporium, Ireland's most exclusive and private members gaming club, in Dublin. And he is a partner with Justin Carthy, in Betchronicle.com.

One of his earliest involvements in racing included having a share in Sound Man, a winner of the Queen Mother Champion Chase in the nineties, trained by Eddie O'Grady.

More recently his famous all white silks with a blue hoop have been carried to success by Commanche Court and Never Compromise. The former won the Triumph Hurdle at the Festival, the Irish Grand National at Fairyhouse and the Heineken Cup at Punchestown. He even got in the place money behind the great Best Mate in Cheltenham's Gold Cup.

At present he has some nice young horses in training with David Wachman. Other trainers he has horses with include Ted Walsh, Christy Roche, Charlie Swan and O'Grady and if one of these gentlemen can provide Desmond with a Cheltenham Gold Cup winner well, that's half of his sporting ambitions achieved.

The other, need you ask, is seeing his beloved Celtic lift the Champions League Trophy. Ask him what his hobbies are and all you'll get is "golf, golf and more golf". Dermot is married to Pat and they have three sons and one daughter.

DERMOT DESMOND

WILLIAM DURKAN

Bill Durkan moved to London from Mayo in the fifties, primarily to look for work. He started out on the building sites as a plasterer before sub-contracting and, as early as 1963 Durkan was building houses in the capital. So the Durkan Construction Company was born and, not only were private houses and social houses being built but also commercial properties. On the odd occasion there would be as many as sixty sites on the go at one time. Over 150 people are employed nowadays in London alone by Durkan and, because he travelled to England at such a young age, he still occasionally refers to London as home even now. But though he continues to clock up the air miles, Durkan has his feet firmly set on Irish soil now.

Perhaps, his love of the racing game has something to do with that.
It was back in the early seventies that Durkan obtained a jockey's licence and rode in point-to-points.

Soon after he acquired the brilliant NH mare Anaglog's Daughter and, his first visit to the Cheltenham festival in 1980 brought success in the Arkle Chase.

Since that introduction to ownership Durkan has turned to owning mainly flat horses and in 2006 the highly successful Miss Beatrix, trained by Kevin Prendergast, won the Moyglare Stud Stakes (G1) and the Goffs Million, both at the Curragh. Other trainers used by Durkan include Mick Halford, P. Prendergast, Charlie Swan, Tom Taaffe, Tom Hogan.

Other than enjoying watching his famous his blue and white silks being worn at Galway, Leopardstown and the Curragh, Durkan loves nothing more than going back to Mayo, taking it easy, admiring the countryside and spending as much time as possible with his family. He has a wife, Beatrice, nine children, five boys and four girls but unfortunately, son John passed away in 1998 after suffering with leukaemia.

WILLIAM DURKAN

MICHAEL FUTTER

When Mike Futter was vice-president at Blackpool Student's Union he used to run a book even though there was a bookmaker's around the corner. Studies ? More like studying the Sporting Life for young Futter.

In 1978, Mike left his beloved Lancashire seaside town for Northern Ireland and thus, began his love of attending point-to-point meetings and horse racing in general.

The attraction of the sport to Futter was to get more involved and this he did with the purchase of horses being the next step. And Monty's Pass was one such point-to-pointer he bought. Indeed he was one of many that contributed to the 110 plus winners that Futter's horses have recorded. To fund his love of the sport Futter only ever used money he had won from bookmakers to purchase the horses.

Mike had a theory that horses running consistently over three miles and carrying 12st in the saddle would be much more likely to reproduce their form on a regular basis, thus giving him as a punter a better-than-average chance of winning.

About 18 months before that memorable day at Aintree in 2003, there was a race where Monty's Pass came up against Moscow Express (rated 30lb superior) and suffered a short-head defeat. And for that loss Monty got raised a whopping 16lb by the handicapper. So, during the following year Monty never managed to trouble the judge again and his weight duly came down. When the weights were issued for the Grand National, Futter then realised Monty had a good racing weight. All he needed now was good ground and the sun on his back, as well as a very good jockey (Barry Geraghty was booked). Everything fell into place on that memorable day in Liverpool and all that was left to do, was to go and collect.

Several bets were struck by Futter at all odds from 66/1 down to 16/1 culminating in a £1.1 million pay-out including the prize money.

On the business front, Mike opened the first commercial bingo hall in Northern Ireland twenty years ago and, promptly sat down with Chris Patten to discuss the legalisation of bingo halls in the north. Following those successful discussions, Futter went on to own seven in the north and another three in Dublin.

A professional gambler through and through, he admits to virtually betting on any sport apart from basketball.

Mike is married to Janet and they have three daughters, Paula, Joanna and Danielle.

Michael Futter

John Magnier

John Magnier is Ireland's leading thoroughbred stud owner and also has various business interests outside of the horse breeding industry. He has also been a senator in the Irish Parliament.

John had to leave school at the age of 15 upon the death of his father, to take charge of the family farm just outside the town of his birth, Fermoy in County Cork.

Coolmore Stud at Fethard, Co.Tipperary is his base and there are also Coolmore farms in Kentucky, USA and New South Wales, Australia.

His association with Coolmore began with his father-in-law and champion racehorse trainer, Vincent O'Brien, and pools magnate Robert Sangster. Between them they developed the best racehorses and breeding stock, primarily by purchasing the progeny of the all-time great stallion, Northern Dancer.

When Magnier came to head the operation, an upward spiral of success was about to begin. His racing empire, the most successful on earth, are trained at Ballydoyle by Aidan O'Brien (no relation to his father-in-law). But there are also many other trainers privileged to have some of Magnier's blue-blooded thoroughbreds within their stables.

At Coolmore, the incomparable Sadler's Wells has been champion sire of Europe on 14 occasions. More recently, notable Group One winners like Giant's Causeway, Galileo and Montjeu, who is now emerging as the probable successor to Sadler's Wells, have been successful in their stud duties.

It is said that John Magnier is the most influential man in horseracing and breeding worldwide, even more so than Sheikh Mohammed bin Rashid Al Maktoum

Away from the equine business, Magnier has proved to be an astute investor and with close friends, J.P.McManus and Dermot Desmond, they have enjoyed phenomenal success.

John is married to Susan, the daughter of Vincent O'Brien, and the couple have five children, Tom, John Paul, Michael, Sam and Katie. While the sons have made their mark within the business, Katie married trainer David Wachman in 2002.

JOHN MAGNIER

J.P. McManus

John Patrick McManus, legendary gambler and racehorse owner is a very proud native of Limerick. And his famous green an gold colours are also those of his home town GAA club, South Liberties.

Owner of more than 100 racehorses, nearly all of them are jumpers. The most famous hurdler of the current era was the now retired Istabraq. Bought by Timmy Hyde for JP for nearly £40k from Sheikh Hamdan al Maktoum he had an illustrious eight year career winning the Smurfit Champion Hurdle in '98, '99 and 2000 and the AIG Champion Hurdle on four occasions plus another 12 Group races. Trained by Aidan O'Brien he was ridden by Charlie Swan.

There was never really a great connection with horses when McManus was a young boy and, on leaving school he worked at his family's plant hire firm until he was 20. He then entered the world of gambling (not that he hadn't had a bet before then) by standing at his local greyhound track as an on-course bookmaker.

His big money gambles soon became well-known and Mister Donovan in 1982 at Cheltenham, was probably his first major hit, winning him £250,000. 15 years later McManus teamed up with his good friend, Dermot Desmond, to purchase Sandy Lane Hotel in Barbados which reputedly cost £38m.

Not only has gambling on horses contributed to the wealth of this quiet and generous gentleman but most of it has come from his trading in foreign currency.

J.P. now lives in Switzerland but he never forgets his roots. He regularly makes visits to the racing festivals and golf tournaments including his own, the J.P.McManus Golf Classic first held in Limerick in 1990. His proudest moment came when he defeated Tiger Woods 3&2 in a head-to-head at Limerick Golf Club. He also partnered British Open winner Padraig Harrington to victory in the Dunhill Links Championship in Scotland.

He has his horses running in Ireland, the UK and France and one of his most recent stars was Baracouda, twice Stayers Hurdle Champion and twice runner-up.

Even with all his success worldwide, McManus would dearly love to see his beloved Limerick win an all-Ireland senior hurling title, something they haven't done since 1973.

J.P. McManus

Michael O'Leary

Michael O'Leary, the oldest in a family of six, was born in Kanturk, County Cork.
He was DCE of Ryanair for three years before being promoted to chief executive in 1994 but, in the early eighties, he was working behind a bar at an uncle's hotel to help fund his studies at Trinity College. In the period between, O'Leary worked as an accountant, owned two newsagents and was also hired as a personal financial and tax advisor to Tony Ryan, head of Guinness Peat Aviation.

O'Leary has often been described as controversial and arrogant and his no-nonsense management style, extreme cost-cutting and meanness towards staff, and scathing criticisms of competitors, governments and unions have become his hallmark.

In 2004 he purchased a hackney plate for his own car, a Mercedes, to enable it to be classified as a taxi so that he could legally make use of the country's bus lanes.

He lives in Gigginstown House near Mullingar in Westmeath with his wife Anita, whom he married in 2003, and their two young sons, Matt and Luke.

O'Leary breeds Aberdeen Angus cattle as well as horses at his Gigginstown House Stud.

His steeplechaser, War Of Attrition, trained by 'Mouse' Morris and ridden by Conor O'Dwyer, won the Cheltenham Gold Cup and the Punchestown Guinness Gold Cup in 2006. The following season injury forced the bay gelding to miss the defence of his Cheltenham crown.

O'Leary's famous maroon and white silks can frequently be seen being carried to victory around Ireland's racecourses.

MICHAEL O'LEARY

LADY CHRYSS O'REILLY

Lady Chryss O'Reilly's maiden name was Goulandris and her cousin, Peter, has had horses in training for many years in the UK under the Hesmond Stud banner. It was Peter who, along with his father, took Chryss to the races in their native homeland of Greece.

As well as thoroughbreds, Arabs were also raced there and the family soon knew which horses 'to be on'.

An uncle, Costa Goulandris, had a stud farm La Louviere in Normandy but when he died in 1978, it was left to Chryss to take over and manage.

Lady Chryss O'Reilly has horses running in her famous black and white hoops with blue cap, in five different countries on both sides of the world but, most predominantly in Ireland and France, where she has eleven trainers in each of those countries racing her horses.

She has had twelve homebred Group One winners including Arc victor, Helissio, Prix du Jockey Club winner Lawman, Bluemamba, Priolo and Latice but only one Group One winner was purchased and owned by Lady O'Reilly. That was Rebelline in the Tattersalls Gold Cup, trained by Kevin Prendergast and ridden by Declan McDonagh. The filly also won the Gladness Stakes and Mooresbridge Stakes during the same year.

The breeding operation which O'Reilly owns, incorporates 130 broodmares split between Castlemartin Stud in Kildare and the Haras de la Louviere in Normandy. Besides the aforementioned stud farms, O'Reilly also has properties in Cork, Deauville and Nassau.

She also employs four trainers in France for her trotting horses.

Favourite racecourses are Chantilly (for its sheer beauty), Longchamp and The Curragh.

Chryss's interests are pedigrees and away from racing she enjoys walking, cycling and the arts.

She married Sir Anthony O'Reilly, an Irish billionaire, in 1991.

LADY CHRYSS O'REILLY

Michael Ryan

A larger than life character in every way, Michael Ryan didn't get involved in racehorse ownership until 1983 when, he was invited by a group of friends to have a one-twelfth share in a horse called Friendly Circle.

Ryan was a familiar face on the local point-to-point scene and his love of racing quickly grew, especially the jumping game.

One of the most popular mares in training, the seven year old Al Eile, trained by John Queally in Ryan's home town of Dungarvan, has won three times at Aintree and twice at Leopardstown including the November Handicap.

In recent years he has acquired a few more horses to run on the flat and over jumps using the services of such trainers as Jim Bolger, Aidan O'Brien and Ted Walsh to name but a few.

In 2007 his amazing filly, Finsceal Beo, carried his famous dark blue and green colours to victory in the English and Irish 1,000 Guineas and, she was only pipped on the line in the French version at Longchamp by the wonder filly, Darjina.

Ryan has travelled all over the world watching racing, the Breeders' Cup every year, Dubai, Melbourne, Hong Kong but he openly admits nothing compares with race week in September at Listowel.

When quizzed whether his ambition was to win the Irish Derby or Cheltenham Gold Cup, the big fella quipped, "no, my dream is to win the Kerry National".

Away from the racing Ryan loves to go fishing and supporting the hurlers of his home county, Waterford.

He has three grown up children, Vanessa, Clodagh and Micheal.

MICHAEL RYAN

Trainers

Jim Bolger

Jim Bolger began showjumping after leaving school. He also had a very short career as an amateur jockey but alas, a very impressive strike rate of 25% (3 from 12).

Bolger's training career commenced at the age of 34 and it wasn't too long before he moved to his present stables at Glebe House, Coolcullen where he has lived and worked for the last 25 years.

During this period Bolger has had such brilliant fillies as Give Thanks, his first Classic success in the Irish Oaks of 1983, Flame Of Tara, Park Appeal, Park Express, Polonia (seven wins), Noora Abu (twelve wins), Jet Ski Lady and Alexander Goldrun, multiple Group One winner.

One memorable day in the summer of '92 Bolger had five winners on the Curragh including St.Jovite in the Budweiser Irish Derby itself.

More recently though the best two year old colt ever to be under Bolger's care was Teofilo, named after the great Cuban amateur boxer, Teofilo Stevenson but, unfortunately injury struck and he did not make it to the track as a three year old.

Going into the winter of 2006, Bolger's colt was made ante-post favourite for the Newmarket Guineas and the Epsom Derby on the back of an unblemished two year old campaign (5 from 5). He wasn't the only star at Glebe House though, as owner Michael Ryan's filly, Finsceal Beo, went on to win both the English and Irish 1,000 Guineas in emphatic style but, unfortunately got short-headed at Longchamp in the French version.

Bolger's breeding operation centres around his broodmares and, with continued expansion on that front, there are certainly more exciting times ahead for all at Glebe House.

Stable jockey is son-in-law, Kevin Manning and he is backed up by two very good apprentices, David Moran and Martin Harley.

Jim Bolger has a love of most sports but in particular, hurling and football, and he always attends the showjumping at the RDS.

Married to wife, Jackie, they have two married daughters, Una and Fiona and, three grandchildren.

JIM BOLGER

Michael Halford

Born in Newbridge, Co.Kildare, Halford's career began first with the pony club and then, whilst still at school, he went along to John Murphy's to ride out and also to Frank Ennis, who trained the family racehorse.

After leaving school he studied Pedigree Research for two years. Then came the opportunity to become assistant trainer to Noel Meade's stable in Castletown, Co.Meath.

By the time Halford was twenty-one, he was offered the chance to train horses at Birdcatcher Stables in Maddenstown, next door to Con Collins. Within two years he had built Seven Springs Stables in Pollardstown, where he still is to this day.

Well, at the moment that is, because in 2006, Halford bought 60 acres of land near Kildangan Stud to develop a new training establishment. On completion, within the next few months, the new stables will house over 100 horses, have two horse spas, swimming pool, two new gallops including an all-weather one. So the 2007 season is very much a transitional period for the Halfords.

At the start of the current flat campaign though, HH Aga Khan supported Halford by sending a dozen well-bred two year olds to him.

Miss Emma was the first Group winner out of Seven Springs landing the G3 Greenland Stakes and two years later, Miss Sally, won a maiden at Navan in the April before going on to claim four more wins that season, including a Listed and two G3 wins. Other stable stars include Quinmaster and Nick's Nikita.

With all what's going on in the busy Halford household, there is simply not enough time in the day for leisure periods. Louise combines being assistant trainer, amateur jockey and mother to Joshua and Thomas.

Louise has currently ridden four winners, none more impressive than Do The Trick at The Curragh in 2007.

Being born and brought up on The Curragh, Halford harbours one prized ambition, training a Classic winner on his home turf. And you won't get long odds against that happening very soon.

MICHAEL HALFORD

Jessica Harrington

Jessica's introduction to horse racing was inevitable as father was a permit holder and point-to-point rider and brother John was himself an amateur rider. She took up hunting, eventing and show jumping as a child so horse racing seemed the natural progression especially as both father and John also had racehorses.

Home was at Summerhill in Co.Meath before Jessica went to England for seven years. She later returned to Ireland to settle in Moone, Co.Kildare, where she has lived for the last 31 years. Upon on her return she met Johnny and they later married. At the time he had a permit and after a few years, Jessica took over. It was in 1990 that she eventually went full-time and in her first year stabled 15 horses whereas now she has over 100 horses in her care.

Her first big race training success came in the shape of Havaheart, winner of the Irish Lincoln Handicap at the Curragh.

Stable stars over the years have included Oh So Grumpy, Space Trucker (15 wins), Slaney Native, Bust Out, Spirit Leader, Studmaster, Hide The Evidence, Cork All Star and Macs Joy.

But who would have guessed back in 1998 at the Derby Sales, that a virtually unknown four year old would have such a bearing on Jessica's future success. A gentleman by the name of Brian Kearney, had instructed her to find a racehorse for £20,000. This was to be his first venture into racehorse ownership. She went to the sales and came back with Moscow Flyer who, upon his retirement at the age of twelve, had won 26 races (in the black and white colours of Kearney) under National Hunt rules including two Queen Mother Champion Chases at Cheltenham.

There is very little time for relaxation in the Harrington household but Jessica enjoys playing golf and her annual week on the slopes, skiing.

She has two children by an earlier marriage, James and Tara, and two with Johnny, Emma and Kate who, incidentally rode "Moscow" to his final victory at Punchestown.

JESSICA HARRINGTON

MICHAEL HOURIGAN

Michael Hourigan began his apprenticeship with trainer Charlie Weld in 1962 riding nine winners during his five years there. He then decided to try his luck with Commander Crawford in Scotland but whilst there he only managed four winners over the sticks.

Returning to his homeland was the next option for Hourigan and, upon taking out a trainer's licence in 1973, he decidedly thought things could only get better. They did but it took a lot of hard word and dedication. For many years Hourigan wasn't even reaching double figures for winners in a season.

In the mid 80's he took a major gamble and purchased a training yard at Patrickswell, near Limerick.

Now, more than twenty years on, Hourigan has trained two of Ireland's most successful and popular steeplechasers, Doran's Pride, who sadly is no longer with us and Beef Or Salmon. The former was shrewdly placed to win a staggering 29 races in a wonderful career including the 2000 November Handicap on the flat.

"Beef", the present star in the yard, has been ultra-consistent over the last five years recording nineteen victories, ten of them at Grade One level including two Hennessy Gold Cups, two Lexus Chases and an Ericsson Chase. Unfortunately, the chestnut gelding has never been able to cope with the undulations of Cheltenham.

Hourigan also enjoyed phenomenal success with Tropical Lake and King Carew who both had ten wins each to their credit. More recently, the Co.Limerick trainer has some very talented chasers at his Lisaleen stables with the smart Hi Cloy, handicapper A New Story and, the useful novices, Arteea, Mossbank and Church Island all paying their way.

After the early struggles during the seventies, no-one can doubt the ability of Michael Hourigan to develop talented young horses.

Hourigan enjoys going out with the hunt and spending time with his family, wife Anne, and children Michael, Kay, Paul, Laura and Mark.

MICHAEL HOURIGAN

Dessie Hughes

At the age of fourteen and with no experience or family background of horses, Dessie Hughes had made his mind up that he wanted to be a jockey. Having started his apprenticeship with Dan Kirwan and riding a couple of winners, Hughes later transferred across to Willie O'Grady, Eddie's father, to finish his time there. Only one more Flat winner came along before weight began to take its toll and the National Hunt scene was the only way to go.

In fact Hughes had a very successful career as a jockey riding such memorable horses at the Cheltenham Festival as Davy Lad (Royal & SunAlliance Hurdle and the Gold Cup), Monksfield (Champion Hurdle), Chinrullah and Tip The Wink (Arkle Chase) and Bit Of A Jig (Supreme Novices Hurdle).

After breaking his collarbone in 1980 Hughes then decided to hang up his boots and start training, his first stables being at Brownstown.

Hughes wasted no time in kicking off his training career with Light The Wad being the standard bearer in the early eighties.

At the Goffs 2001 Land Rover Sale, Hughes picked up two four year olds for IR£49,000. Incredibly, they went on to be first and second in the Cheltenham Bumper the following year. Now more than five years on, those two horses have won 22 races including eight Grade 1's between them. Who are they ? Hardy Eustace and Central House !

Everyone in racing associates Hughes with the great Hardy Eustace, twice Champion Hurdler in 2004 and 2005 and likely to be aimed at stayers races in future. Other horses Hughes talks about with affection are Schindlers Hunt, Colonel Braxton and his first ever training success, Another Story.

Fairyhouse and Punchestown are his favourite courses.

Married to Eileen, Dessie has two children, Richard, who has been riding Flat winners with great success in the UK for the last twelve years, and Sandra.

Watching racing and golf on the television is how Hughes likes to relax.

DESSIE HUGHES

NOEL MEADE

Noel Meade began training in 1971 with only one horse to his name but gradually a few decent flat horses came into the yard. And seven years on at Royal Ascot in the Cork and Orrery Stakes, Sweet Mint won for Meade and most probably, that was what served the public notice that here was a young man who was destined to go to the top of his profession.

Even though Meade was successfully training under both codes he eventually decided to concentrate primarily on training jumpers, a decision that has since seen him win six consecutive trainers championships.

During the mid 90s Paul Carberry was assigned to ride for Meade as stable jockey and the pair gained immediate success with Johnny Setaside in the Grade One Drinmore Novice Chase.

Meade has also had to endure sadness during the late 90s as well, when the aforementioned collapsed and died after winning the 1996 Ericsson Chase and three years later the loss of Cardinal Hill was undoubtedly the lowest point of Meade's career. The JP McManus owned gelding was a very talented horse and could have reached the very top of his game after impressively winning the 1999 Champion Novice Hurdle at Punchestown. Amazingly though, Noel Meade has only visited the winners enclosure at Cheltenham twice, the first time being with Sausalito Bay in 2000 who beat Best Mate, later to become triple Gold Cup winner at the Festival and, six years later with Nicanor.

Chasers that gave the yard great success were dual Grand National winner The Bunny Boiler and, twice placed in the Gold Cup, Harbour Pilot.

With hurdler Harchibald being touched off in the 2005 Champion Hurdle, Meade doesn't hide the fact that he'd like to win that particular race and the Cheltenham Gold Cup before he retires.

Meade does still house a handful of good flat horses at Castletown, none more so than Arch Rebel, winner of four Listed races.

Outside of racing he's a big follower of Meath football and hurling.

NOEL MEADE

ARTHUR MOORE

Arthur Moore has been equally successful both as a jockey and as a trainer. In the saddle Moore won the 1971 Irish Grand National on King's Sprite and rode Veuve to two big handicaps successes in the 1971 Troytown Chase and the 1973 Thyestes Chase.

But training was always going to be Moore's objective in life having learned his trade from his father, Dan. It was Dan who trained the brilliant chaser, L'Escargot to win the 1970 and 1971 Cheltenham Gold Cup and the 1975 Aintree Grand National, thus preventing the immortal Red Rum from winning three successive Grand Nationals.

In the late seventies Moore acquired Royal Bond who went on to win seventeen times, the last being at the age of fifteen. In 1979 Irian became Moore's first of six winners of the Irish Sweeps Hurdle (now the Pierse Hurdle) at Leopardstown.

Drumgora broke Moore's duck at the Cheltenham Festival winning the 1981 Queen Mother Champion Chase and quickly followed up in 1982 winning the Arkle Chase with The Brockshee.

Feroda and Second Schedual proved to be very talented chasers in the early nineties until the classy Klairon Davis arrived on the scene. Undefeated in his novice hurdling season he went on to collect many graded chases in his career but, the pinnacle was in 1996 when he won the Queen Mother Champion Chase from Viking Flagship and Sound Man.

Two years later, Moore was training Native Upmanship for John Magnier and this "two mile four" specialist, under regular jockey Conor O'Dwyer, earned over €1m in an illustrious career. Unfortunately, for this chestnut gelding, there was never a championship race over his distance at the Festival.

These last few seasons have been relatively quiet for Moore but, with the experience and guile of this genial "gentleman of the turf", it won't be long before he is competitive again in the valuable handicaps at all the major festivals.

ARTHUR MOORE

Joanna Morgan

After spending eight years riding for Seamus McGrath, Joanna then became pregnant. Two daughters and a few years later, when the girls began school, Joanna resumed riding and her career spanned nearly 200 winners in total.

Big handicaps she won included the Cambridgeshire twice, aboard Yankee's Princess and The Bower. But her most notable performance came, when she was four months "in foal again", riding One Won One to victory at Galway. She has also had a mount in the Irish Derby, finishing unplaced. In fact, Joanna has ridden a winner on four different continents.

When Jo began her training career at Dunsany in 1985 she never had more than a handful of horses in her yard. She later moved to larger premises at Ballivor, Co.Meath where One Won One was the real star in the yard, the winner of a Group Three in Ireland and a listed winner in Dubai and owned by the Heavenly Syndicate headed by Fr. Sean Breen. A winner in total of thirteen races.

In fact, Joanna was twice victorious on One Won One prior to her retirement from the saddle.

A more recent and popular servant at Morgan's stables is Portant Fella who amazingly, in 2006, won a two mile novice chase at Roscommon and a seven furlong handicap on the sand at Laytown, both within in 24 hours. Other horses this season that Morgan has seen entering the winner's enclosure are Orpailleur and Jawad.

Relaxation for Jo is sitting in her conservatory reading the Sunday Times and ambitions, in her own words "are to stay alive without fucking hanging myself".

Another Group winner or two and maybe Jo will fulfil her ambition.

Her three children are daughters Katie and Maggie and son, Morgan.

JOANNA MORGAN

Michael 'Mouse' Morris

'Mouse' Morris was an amateur jockey (1969-1975) of immense talent and he came to prominence when riding Mr.Midland to victory in the National Hunt Chase at Cheltenham in 1974. But the highlight of his career came when he rode the durable Skymas to successive wins in the Queen Mother Champion Chase in 1976 and 1977.

During his riding career he rode over 600 winners.

After taking out his trainer's licence in the early eighties, Morris was fortunate to have a very good novice, Buck House, in his yard. After winning the Supreme Novices Hurdle in 1983, the gelding then began to realise his true potential when switched to fences and, in 1986, won the Queen Mother Champion Chase under Tommy Carmody.

Other good horses to come out of Everardsgrange, Co.Tipperary are Cahervillahow, His Song, Foxchapel King, Fota Island, Trapper John, Belvederian and the stable "superstar" War Of Attrition. Owned by Ryanair supremo, Michael O'Leary, the youngest horse in the Gold Cup field of 2006 came up the famous Cheltenham hill 2½ lengths clear of Grand National winner, Hedgehunter.

Unfortunately for connections War Of Attrition picked up a tendon injury just a week before he was due to defend his crown and has been unable to race since.

Morris currently has a string of 45 horses, many of them owned by wealthy businessmen including Sir Anthony O'Reilly, Michael O'Flynn and O'Leary himself.

His favourite racecourse is Cheltenham but away from the business end, Morris likes to go hunting and play golf.

He has two sons, Jamie and Christopher.

MICHAEL 'MOUSE' MORRIS

WILLIE MULLINS

W.P.Mullins was born into racing as his father had been a trainer for many years and, it was just natural that Willie would follow suit. He didn't start riding though until he was seventeen and by the time he hung up his boots, he had amassed over 400 winners.

Replaying his memorable rides, Mullins feels there is no comparison with riding over the fences at Aintree and he won the 1983 Foxhunters Chase on his father's horse Atha Cliath but, also has fond memories of his first ever Cheltenham Festival winner, Hazy Dawn.

Mullins has been training now for twenty years from his yard at Closutton, Co.Carlow and currently stables about 100 horses, of which threequarters would be National Hunt.

Notoriously renowned for readying "bumper" horses, he has won the Cheltenham Festival Bumper on five occasions, once with the mighty Florida Pearl (1997) who, went on to win the Hennessy Gold Cup at Leopardstown four times. In fact, Willie gave up riding after winning on Wither or Which, his own horse and the first of the five, in 1996. Alexander Banquet (1998), Joe Cullen (2000) and Missed That (2005) complete the roll of honour.

Other notable horses to come out of Closutton include Tourist Attraction, the first of nine Festival winners, Rule Supreme, Adamant Approach, Micko's Dream and Holy Orders.

But as any NH trainer will tell you, winning the Aintree Grand National is the pinnacle of one's career and Hedgehunter in 2005 gave Mullins his greatest thrill. Winning another "National" and a group race on the flat are his immediate ambitions but, to go on training for as long as the desire and excitement remains within him, Willie Mullins would more than settle for that.

Away from the races, he enjoys playing golf and watching his beloved Kilkenny hurlers.

Married to Jackie they have one son, Patrick William, who is currently leading amateur jockey in 2007.

WILLIE MULLINS

Aidan O'Brien

Aidan O'Brien enjoyed a brief riding career becoming amateur champion jockey in 1994 before applying for his trainer's licence at the tender age of 23. It wasn't the Flat but National Hunt where O'Brien made his mark as a trainer sending out two winners on his first day and being champion trainer at the end of that season. After his second season, when he broke the record for number of wins in a year, he decided to try his hand training primarily Flat horses.

He was invited by John and Susan Magnier to take over the training operation at the Ballydoyle stables in Co.Tipperary, an establishment with some of the most advanced training facilities in the world. The Magniers with their huge financial backing gave them the ability to compete with the wealthy Arabs at the sales.

In his first year at Ballydoyle, O'Brien sent out 176 winners under both codes which was a record in Ireland until he broke it again the following year.

O'Brien, still only 38, has certainly become the most successful trainer of the modern era.

To date, he has trained the winners of 16 Irish Classics, 13 English Classics and 4 French Classics amongst a total of over 120 Group One winners worldwide.

Great racehorses such as Rock Of Gibraltar (seven consecutive Group One wins), High Chaparral (twice Breeders' Cup winner and dual Derby winner), Galileo, Giant's Causeway and Dylan Thomas, 2007 Arc winner are just some of the equine talent O'Brien has trained but there is one jumper he will always be associated with, the champion hurdler of the late nineties, Istabraq.

Istabraq won 23 races in all, including three Cheltenham Champion Hurdles and four AIG Champion Hurdles at Leopardstown.

Retained jockeys at Ballydoyle are K Fallon, J A Heffernan and C O'Donoghue although Michael Kinane and J P Murtagh are used frequently.

Born in Co.Wexford, Aidan O'Brien is married to Anne-Marie and they have four children, Joseph, Sarah, Anna and Donnacha.

AIDAN O'BRIEN

EDDIE O'GRADY

Edward O'Grady began training in 1972 following on from his father, Willie, who sent out many winners during the 1950s and 1960s. His stables are situated at Ballynonty in Co.Tipperary and his first notable success came via Mr.Midland in the National Hunt Chase at Cheltenham in 1974, in the hands of 'Mouse' Morris, now a successful trainer in his own right and a neighbour of O'Grady's.

It was in 1978 that will always be remembered by O'Grady as a year that depicts the "up and downs" of National Hunt racing. Jack Of Trumps, owned by J.P.McManus, landed four chases including the Heineken Gold Cup. But that year will always be known as Golden Cygnet's year. Following a twenty length win in a maiden hurdle, a few days before the turn of the year, O'Grady's gelding went on to win at Naas and Punchestown before landing the Supreme Novices Hurdle at Cheltenham by no less than 15 lengths. After another victory, this time at Fairyhouse, saw Golden Cygnet pitched in at the deep end at Ayr for the Scottish Champion Hurdle. Coming to the last alongside the great Sea Pigeon, he took a crashing fall and was killed outright leaving many unfulfilled dreams and broken hearts as the racing public looked on in horror. This horse had the potential to be one of the all-time greats and, for O'Grady and jockey Niall Madden this had to be the worst day of their respective careers.

The following year saw O'Grady bounce back with the big race double at the Galway Festival in the shape of Hindhope and Hard Tarquin, a feat that's not been achieved since.

Two years later and he was beginning to train more flat horses and duly saddled his first group winner, Cooleen Jack, in the Ballyogan Stakes. 1983 saw Bit Of A Skite win the National Hunt Chase and the Irish Grand National.

Other notable horses to bring big race success to O'Grady include Nick Dundee, Ned Kelly, Time For A Run, Back In Front, Pizarro and Sky's The Limit.

EDDIE O'GRADY

JOHN OXX

John Oxx began training from his Currabeg stables in Kildare in 1979 and, is without doubt, one of Ireland's most successful trainers over the last 20 years.

His first Classic success came when Eurobird ran out a decisive winner of the '87 Irish St. Leger and within two years he won the same race again, this time with Petite Ile in the hands of top Aussie jockey, Ron Quinton.

The following year saw HH Aga Khan transfer many of his horses to Oxx and with it, many Classics were to be won at home and abroad.

The horse that made the racing public sit up and take notice of John's training talents was the brilliant filly, Ridgewood Pearl, who in 1995 won the Irish 1000 Guineas, the Coronation Stakes, the Prix du Moulin and the Breeders' Cup Mile. Four Group One wins in four different countries plus the Athasi Stakes made her achievements a truly outstanding feat.

In 2000, the magnificent Sinndar became the first horse to win the Irish Derby, the Epsom Derby and the Prix de l'Arc de Triomphe in the same year which also culminated in stable jockey Johnny Murtagh winning twelve G1's in that year. An unbelievable season for top jockey, Murtagh.

Oxx has in fact won eight Classics in his home country.

One filly who didn't win a Classic but did record ten victories, including three G1's in '95 and '96 was Timarida. Her victory in the Champion Stakes was particularly memorable. Other fillies to bring success to Currabeg were the '97 and '98 Irish Oaks winners, Ebadiyla and Winona.

In the first decade of the new century, Alamshar, Azamour and Kastoria all won major races for Oxx and HH Aga Khan. What a memorable race the 2003 Irish Derby threw up, with Dalakhani (C.Soumillon) and Alamshar (J.Murtagh) going neck and neck inside the final quarter until Murtagh's mount got up on the line to edge out the odds-on French colt.

The Oxx and Murtagh partnership came to an amicable split and the post of stable jockey was accepted by the "old master", Mick Kinane.

John is married to Caitriona and they have three children, Deirdre, Aoife and Kevin.

JOHN OXX

KEVIN PRENDERGAST

Kevin Prendergast was an amateur jockey for a few years before taking out his trainer's licence in the 1960's. Many of the top jockeys in Ireland served their apprenticeship under the guidance of Prendergast. The current champion Declan McDonagh and twice apprentice champion, Chris Hayes, are the stable jockeys at Friarstown.

Pidget gave Kevin his first Classic success when winning the Irish 1000 Guineas in 1972 and this very classy filly when on to claim another Classic later that year, the Irish St.Leger.

Indeed, the all-aged Classic has proved to be a lucky race for Kevin over the years having won it with Conor Pass in 1973 and with dual winner Oscar Schindler in 1996 and 1997.

The latter also won the Hardwicke Stakes and the Ormonde Stakes on his travels to the UK in '96 and, was placed twice in the '96 and '97 runnings of the Prix de l'Arc de Triomphe.

In 1996 Verglas was another winner for Prendergast, this time at the Royal Ascot meeting in the Coventry Stakes, a race his father 'Darkie' had won on six occasions.

Other important successes over the years have included four Pretty Polly Stakes with Pidget ('72), Lady Singer ('76), Polaire ('99) and Rebelline (2002), and the Gladness Stakes on five occasions courtesy of Rare Appeal ('77), Lidhame ('86), Secret of Success ('79), Rebelline (2002) and Mustameet (2005).

Prendergast enjoyed more Classic success in the Irish 2000 Guineas with Northern Treasure (76) and a year later won his only English Classic, the 2000 Guineas with Nebbiolo. Arctique Royale gave him another Irish 1000 Guineas victory in 1981.

Kevin is still going strong and more than forty years on from taking out his licence, the winners continue to flow. Mustameet, winner of five races in 2006 and Miss Beatrix, winner of the Moyglare Stud Stakes and the inaugural running of the Shelbourne Hotel Goffs Million Race in the same year are proof that Prendergast is still at the top of his game.

KEVIN PRENDERGAST

CHRISTY ROCHE

Christy Roche, renowned as one of Ireland's best ever flat jockeys, won three Budweiser Irish Derby's on Assert ('82), St.Jovite ('92) and Desrt King ('97) and, also gained a short head success aboard Secreto in the 1984 Epsom Derby amongst his total of 14 Classic winners.

He was seven times Irish Champion jockey prior to hanging up his boots and, was primarily associated with the late Paddy Prendergast, David O'Brien and Jim Bolger.

Roche retired from the saddle in 1998 having already taken out a trainer's licence a couple of years earlier. Nowadays, jumpers rather than the flat racers are his passion.

During the last ten years, Roche has enjoyed much success and his main patron, J.P.McManus has supported him from the outset. One of their early successes was Grimes, who won nine races including the 2001 Galway Plate.

His first Cheltenham Festival winner was Khayrawani in the 1999 Coral Cup but who could ever forget his next two, Like-A-Butterfly and Youlneverwalkalone. The latter won ten races in total including the Grade One Hatton's Grace Hurdle and the 2003 William Hill Handicap Chase under Barry Geraghty.

The mare, Like-A-Butterfly was probably the best horse he has ever trained, recording 12 wins in a brilliant career including the 2002 Supreme Novices Hurdle and the 2003 AIG Europe Champion Hurdle. Roche has enjoyed further success with the likes of Bannow Bay, Risk Assessor, Calladine, Wouldn't You Agree, Le Coudray and Far From Trouble, who between them recorded more than forty victories. Calladine also landed the November Handicap at Leopardstown in 2001.

Christy is married to Noeleen and has two sons, William and Padraigh.

CHRISTY ROCHE

TOMMY STACK

Mention Tommy Stack and you think of Red Rum and memories of that April afternoon in 1977 at Aintree coming flooding back.

Tommy was born in Moyvane, Co.Kerry nearly 62 years ago and, his love of horses as a boy were becoming more evident with the time he spent with a piebald pony on the family farm.

At Mungret College he was a very talented scrum-half and played for the Munster schoolboys' rugby team. While there he met Barry Brogan, another jump jockey of the future and, would go to his father's stables to ride out. Stack would try and model himself on past 'greats' Pat Taaffe and Bobby Beasley.

Bobby Renton, a cattle dealer and racehorse trainer from Ripon, North Yorkshire gave Stack his first break in racing and as an amateur, he gained his first win aboard New Money at Wetherby in October, 1965 Who'd have thought less than twelve years later Tommy would be riding into sporting history aboard the great Red Rum, the winner of three Aintree Grand Nationals and runner-up in two.

He was champion jockey on two occasions.

At 32 Stack decided to quit riding and take out a trainer's licence.

In Las Meninas, Tommy unearthed a top class filly who won the English 1000 Guineas and was narrowly beaten by Mehthaaf in the Irish equivalent.

Four years later and another Classic winner came out of his Co.Tipperary stable in the form of Tarascon, under Jamie Spencer winning the Irish 1000 Guineas.

Other notable racehorses that Stack has had the fortune to train include Corwyn Bay, Single Combat, Clean Cut, Kostroma, Tolpuddle and Drayton.

Unfortunately, tragedy struck on St.Stephen's Day in 1998 when Tommy was diagnosed with Meningitis. He spent 13 days unconscious on a life-support machine and two months in hospital overall. Recovery was a long, slow process but in typical fighting spirit, Tommy came through.

And hopefully, his latest two-year old star, Myboycharlie will bring more fortune (of the good sort) to the Stack family.

TOMMY STACK

CHARLIE SWAN

Charlie Swan was born in Modreeny to parents Donald and Theresa. Though his parents were born in England, father trained racehorses at their stables in Modreeny and son Charlie has carried on the tradition with reasonable success.

Swan was riding ponies as soon as he was walking and became quite a competitor at the gymkhanas and show jumping. His father took him racing when he was 13 and he soon got the bug for wanting to ride at speed.

On leaving school, he went to Kevin Prendergast to serve his apprenticeship. He had ridden nearly 80 winners and was lying second in the apprentice championship when an unfortunate accident schooling over hurdles left him with a broken leg. On his return from injury his weight had increased and that left him with no option but to ride over the jumps.

When you mention Charlie Swan you automatically think of the great Istabraq. They were invincible as a team. Istabraq was triple Champion Hurdler at the Cheltenham Festival in 1998, 1999 and 2000 and, quite possibly robbed of a fourth hurdling crown with the "foot and mouth" outbreak forcing the cancellation of the 2001 meeting. Other great hurdlers Swan rode included Danoli and Montelado. Another highlight of his riding career was the victory on board Viking Flagship in the 1995 Queen Mother Champion Chase.

Charlie Swan was champion jockey in Ireland for 10 consecutive years from 1989 and top jockey at the Festival on two occasions.

While still riding over hurdles, Swan took out his trainer's licence in 1998 and saddled his first winner, Fawn Prince, at Bellewstown in July of that year. He continued to combine riding and training for another five years before finally hanging up his boots.

Now fully recognised as one of Ireland's leading NH trainers, Swan has 80 plus horses in his stables, many for J.P.McManus the owner of Istabraq, who has maintained his support for Swan.

Playing golf and cricket and watching rugby are hobbies that he enjoys but, with a young family and a busy career there doesn't appear to be enough hours in the day for Swan.
Married to Carol, he has three children David, Harry and Olivia.

CHARLIE SWAN

TOM TAAFFE

Tom Taaffe is the son of Pat Taaffe, who rode the legendary Arkle to win three successive Cheltenham Gold Cups in the 60s.

Tom himself enjoyed a fine career as a jockey, riding 400 winners, and his partnership with trainer Arthur Moore yielded plenty of winners, most notably in the Pierse Hurdle at Leopardstown in 1983/84/86/88. Fredcoteri, who obliged in '83 and '84 won the AIG Champion Hurdle the following year under Taaffe. He also rode Brittany Boy to victory in the Irish Grand National in 1987.

In 1994 Taaffe took out his trainer's licence and set up at Portree Stables just outside Straffan in Co.Kildare.

One of his earliest big winners was Delphi Lodge (seven wins in total) who won the Power Gold Cup and Fortria Chase in 1998. Mr.Baxter Basics won eight times in the late nineties and Emotional Moment, who won his first race in 2001 and a great servant to Taaffe, has now won twelve times and amassed over €300,000 in prize money.

The smart Tumbling Dice and Secret Native have notched up thirteen successes between them and Cane Brake achieved a remarkable double in 2006, winning both the William Hill Troytown Chase and the Paddy Power Chase, the latter being under top weight on heavy ground.

Whenever available, jockey Barry Geraghty is the preferred choice for Taaffe.

The undoubted star at Portree in recent years has been the Conor Clarkson owned Kicking King, from winning a bumper at Leopardstown in 2002 to winning the ultimate prize, the Cheltenham Gold Cup in 2005. He also won consecutive King George VI chases in 2004 and 2005 and a Punchestown Gold Cup among his Grade One successes but, sadly he sustained a career threatening injury in the second of his King George's.

Tom Taaffe has certainly proved himself to be one of Ireland's finest NH trainers of this generation.

Elaine, his wife, and sons Pat and Alex complete the Taaffe family.

TOM TAAFFE

TED WALSH

Ted Walsh was born into racing as his father and uncle, both publicans, were also horse dealers in Co.Cork. They eventually threw their hat into the ring and bought a yard in Fermoy, where Ted was born, specifically for training point-to-pointers. Horses would also be got ready for the Dublin Horse Show, hunters got ready for their season and other horses sold to England. They probably ended up doing more dealing than training.

In the late fifties, Walsh moved to a yard in Chapelizod for a short spell before settling at Kill near Goffs, where he still trains.

Notable successes during his riding career included Attitude Adjuster in the 1976 hunter chase at Cheltenham, Hilly Way three years later in the Queen Mother Champion Chase and Daring Run in both the 1981 and 1982 Irish Champion Hurdle.

Walsh rode for nearly twenty years before retiring. Father was still alive at that time so Walsh became very keen to help out within the yard. Later that year he was invited to do some television work, again something Walsh has proved very adept at and, watching the major racing festivals throughout Ireland and the UK without him at the "mike", certainly wouldn't seem the same.

In 1991 father passed away and Ted automatically took over the licence.

The highlight of Walsh's career came in 2000 when son, Ruby, won the Aintree Grand National aboard the horse he trained, Papillon.

Other stable stars over the years have been Commanche Court, Rince Ri, True Blue Victory, Never Compromise, Bob Justice and Southern Vic.

Like Walsh says "I've had some good horses over the years but, I would like to train one great horse before I retire"

Married to his childhood sweetheart Helen, they have four children, two sons Ruby and Ted and, two daughters Jennifer and Katie.

Ruby is the most successful National Hunt jockey in Ireland of the modern era and Katie is a very talented amateur rider.

TED WALSH

DERMOT WELD

One of Weld's first recollections of racing was accompanying his father, as a young child, leading in the winner of the Galway Plate, Highfield Lad. From then on Ballybrit racecourse has always meant a lot to the Weld family.

At the age of fifteen, young Dermot had his first ride in public at Ballinrobe and a week later, he rode Ticonderoga to land the amateur riders race (Players Wills H'cap) on the Monday of the Galway Festival. 44 years on from that memorable first success and Weld trained the winner of the same amateur race in the shape of Loyal Focus (2007). Weld went on to become three times amateur champion jockey of Ireland with a strike rate of over 30% of winners to rides.

Weld also trained and rode the winner of the Moet & Chandon Amateurs Derby at Epsom, he rode the winner of the South African Champion Hurdle and also top amateur races in France and the US as well.

In all, Weld had chalked up over 500 winners wordwide as an amateur jockey and he also became the youngest veterinary surgeon in the world at the age of 21, after qualification from the UCD. Immediately, he took up a position in the States as a vet and then moved on to Australia before returning to Ireland to train full time, after the death of his father. Still only 23 years old, young Weld had become the master of Rosewell House.

Now, many years on, there have been 21 European Classic winners come out of Rosewell including Grey Swallow and Zagreb (Irish Derby), Blue Wind (Epsom Oaks) and Vinnie Roe (Irish St.Leger in four consecutive years). On the National Hunt scene, Weld has won four Galway Plates, three Galway Hurdles, an Irish and a Kerry National, and an Irish Champion Hurdle. Weld also became the first and only European trainer to have won the Melbourne Cup, on two occasions now, with Vintage Crop and Media Puzzle.

Of all the racecourses worldwide, Flemington, Galway, Leopardstown and The Curragh would be at the top of Weld's list.

An avid sportsman, he played rugby at university and nowadays he enjoys watching soccer, golf, GAA and rugby.

Married to Mary, he has two sons Mark and Chris.

DERMOT WELD

JOCKEYS

NINA CARBERRY

Nina Carberry, arguably recognised as the leading lady jockey in Ireland, began her career pony riding in 1995 and five years later she took out an amateur jockey's licence. Her first ride in public was on one of father Tommy's horses, she came third.

In 2001, Carberry joined top NH trainer Noel Meade at his Castletown Stables and, won the Ladies Derby at the Curragh in July of that year aboard Sabrinsky. And that, when she was only sixteen. In such a short space of time, she has ridden nearly 100 winners. She has twice rode a winner at the Cheltenham Festival, Dabiroun for trainer Paul Nolan and Heads On The Ground for Enda Bolger in the 2007 Sporting Index Cross Country Chase.

With her career taking off, Nina is very happy to be riding "for the best yard in the country" and, admits it would have to be a very special offer to prise her away from Castletown. Most of the young horses at Meade's she gets to sit on but after their "bumper" runs it's generally left to brother Paul to ride them over hurdles. One such talented horse she speaks highly of is Aran Concerto.

Nina has a great tactical brain and natural talent and in 2006 she became Champion Amateur. In her relatively short career so far, Nina has guided such horses to victory as Solerina, Mansony, Celestial Wave, General Striker, Leading Run and Mick The Man.

Tommy, her father has trained a Grand National winner, Bobbyjo, ridden by brother Paul and, her other brother Philip has ridden the winner of Irish Grand National, Point Barrow in 2006 so competition is very much alive in the Carberry household. As Nina is quick to point out though, "we are all there to support each other".

Her favourite racecourses are Galway, Punchestown and Fairyhouse.
One day Aintree may be included in that list.

Away from the horses, Nina likes to spend as much time as possible surfing and swimming.

NINA CARBERRY

PAUL CARBERRY

Paul Carberry loved nothing more than going hunting and, this is while he was still at school. Soon after his education days were finished though, another education was to begin, his apprenticeship under Jim Bolger at Coolcullen, Co.Kilkenny. He stayed there for three years before moving to his present governor at Castletown, Noel Meade, although he did have a spell riding Mr.Robert Ogden's horses in England.

His first flat winner for Bolger was at Leopardstown in 1990 on a filly called Petronelli but rising weight forced him to give up flat racing.

A supremely confident jockey, Paul's quiet and often motionless manner of riding make it very easy for commentator and racegoer alike to spot him in a race.

His first Cheltenham Festival winner came aboard Rhythm Section in the bumper in 1993. Other Festival winners include Looks Like Trouble (1999 Sun Alliance Chase) who, the following year won the "Blue Riband", Sausalito Bay (2000 Supreme Novices Hurdle), Nicanor (2006 Sun Alliance Novice Hurdle) and Hairy Molly (2006 Champion Bumper).
In 1998 Carberry rode his father's (Tommy) horse, Bobbyjo, to win the Irish Grand National but the highlight of his career came the following spring when steering the same horse to victory in the Aintree Grand National. The scenes of celebration that followed had never been seen before as Paul swung from the rafters in the winners' circle.

Carberry has been Champion NH Jockey on two occasions, in 2002 and 2003 and, has ridden some of Ireland's finest including the late Doran's Pride, Florida Pearl, Beef Or Salmon, Limestone Lad, Harchibald and Aran Concerto.

Tommy is still training at Ratoath, Co.Meath and brother Philip and sister Nina are both talented and competent riders in their own right. But ask Paul what he likes doing away from racing and you'll get a rapid one-word answer.................. hunting!

Paul has two children, Lauren aged nine and Joshua aged seven.

PAUL CARBERRY

KIEREN FALLON

Arguably, Kieren Fallon is one of the all-time greats and one would find it hard to believe that this superb horseman had never even sat on the back of a horse until he was seventeen. In his own words he was "5st fully dressed" and, that was then when Des Scahill, the Irish racing commentator introduced Fallon to Kevin Prendergast, one of Ireland's leading trainers.

Fallon spent three years as apprentice to Prendergast before crossing the water to team up with Jimmy Fitzgerald at Malton, North Yorkshire and later, spent three great years with Linda and Jack Ramsden. As a talent, Fallon was beginning to get recognised by the top trainers in the south and was soon offered the job as stable jockey to the incomparable and highly successful, Henry Cecil. His first classic victory came aboard Sleepytime in 1997 1,000 Guineas at Newmarket. Since then he has gone on to ride another thirteen English Classic winners plus numerous other Group One's in Ireland, France and throughout the world. In all, he was champion jockey in England on six occasions.

After his controversial split with Cecil, he stayed in Newmarket to join Sir Michael Stoute before "an offer I couldn't refuse" came along, to join the team at Ballydoyle. For the Irish genius it was the chance to ply his trade in front of his army of fans back home.

Now, in his forties and riding better than ever, Fallon lists among his great racehorses to have ridden, Dylan Thomas, George Washington and Holy Roman Emperor.

One thing about Fallon that stands out is his appreciation and grateful thanks to those who have supported him during the turbulent times of his career and the controversy caused by the media's intrusion into his private life.
The price of success one might say. "Special thanks", he says, go to his present retainers, John Magnier, Michael Tabor and Derrick Smith.

Away from the track, Kieren enjoys playing golf and squash, in fact any sport competitively.

And who'd back against his son, young Cieren age 8, becoming a future champion jockey. His family is completed by his two daughters, Natalie and Britney.

KIEREN FALLON

Kevin Manning

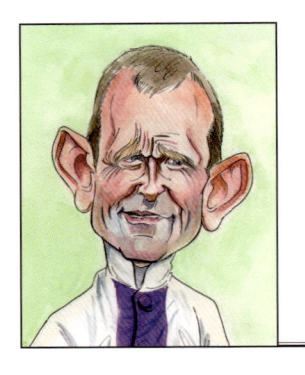

Kevin Manning was brought up in Kilsallaghan, North Co.Dublin and at the age of nine was frequently going racing with his father. His parents bought him his first pony and progression was through show jumping to the time of his apprenticeship with Jim Bolger who, was later to become his father-in-law.

Manning became Champion Apprentice in 1987 with 33 winners, defeating Kieren Fallon, who subsequently went on to become six times English Champion Jockey.

Happily married with wife, Una and children James and Clare, Kevin has had no ambitions to uproot the family and try his luck in the UK.

Why would he want to quit his homeland when father-in-law Jim has one of the strongest stables in Ireland and, Manning himself has had phenomenal success riding equine stars such as Finsceal Beo, dual 1,000 Guineas winner of 2007 and Teofilo, the all conquering two year old of 2006. The fact that Teofilo didn't make the track as a three year old (due to injury) must have been heartbreaking for all concerned.

Two year old colt New Approach looks like the new star out of Coolcullen, Manning remains unbeaten on him after five impressive wins.

Amazingly, Manning has rode only one other horse to classic glory and that was the filly Margarula in the Irish Oaks of 2002.

Indeed, Manning has had tremendous success with fillies during his career. Noora Abu, Eva Luna, Marionnaud, Dazzling Park and Tropical Lady were very classy fillies but, probably none more so than Alexander Goldrun on whom Kevin rode to victory on no less than ten occasions, five of them at Group One level in four different countries.

Away from the track Manning loves nothing more than to spend time at home with his family. Gardening and shooting are pastimes he tries to make time for.

Following in the family footsteps of training are not on Manning's agenda and he is more than happy to continue doing what he does best, riding well and more importantly, riding winners.

KEVIN MANNING

Tony McCoy

Tony McCoy, the greatest jump jockey of all time, was born on 4 May 1974 in Moneyglass, County Antrim.

What is remarkable about McCoy is his physique, 1.80m tall and can get down to 145lbs on the scales. Yet there is no more powerful man in a finish.

He rode his first winner, Legal Steps, at Thurles in March 1992 and within two years he made the move across to England. In his first season he won the conditional jockeys championship with a record 74 winners and, what followed was the remarkable feat of twelve successive jockeys championships.

McCoy landed the Cheltenham big race double in 1997, riding Make A Stand to win the Champion Hurdle for his guv'nor, Martin Pipe, and Mr.Mulligan, from the Noel Chance yard, to win the Gold Cup.

During the 2001/02 season McCoy booted home 289 winners and to date has ridden more than 2,600 winners in his career. In the August of that season McCoy surpassed Richard Dunwoody's record of all time NH winners when winning on Mighty Montefalco at Uttoxeter.

Four months later, at Kempton's Christmas meeting, Tony got the call from Jim Lewis to ride the great Best Mate in the King George and duly won. In fact, he won the Queen Mother Champion Chase on Lewis' Edredon Bleu in 2000, in what was an epic finish up the Cheltenham hill.

When arriving from Ireland McCoy rode for top trainer Martin Pipe, based at Nicholashayne in Somerset, before moving on to ride for his present retainer, Irish millionaire J.P.McManus and his trainer, Jonjo O'Neill. In fact, he rode his first Irish Grand National winner in 2007 at Fairyhouse on board Butler's Cabin, for JP.

There are few ambitions left for this genius in the saddle but, before ending his riding career, he would dearly like to win the Aintree Grand National and, also to ride 300 winners in a season. The nearest he has come to achieving the former was in 2001, '02 and '06 when he was third on each occasion.

He has already written two autobiographies, Real McCoy : My Life So Far in 1999 and McCoy in 2003.

TONY McCOY

DECLAN MCDONAGH

Declan's father was training horses just outside Kells, Co.Meath, and it was a natural progression for young Declan to be introduced into the game. After initially riding ponies, he began working for his father and he was only fifteen when he rode his first winner, Aines Pet.

During his apprenticeship he rode work two days a week for Dermot Weld before going on to work for Kevin Prendergast and eventually losing his claim in 1999.

In only his seventh full season riding as a pro, he became champion jockey with 89 winners to his credit. Notable winners during his Championship season include Miss Beatrix in the Goffs Million, Decado, Mustameet (winner of five stakes races) and Elhamri, his first Royal Ascot winner. McDonagh was also crowned leading jockey that year at both the Galway and Listowel Festivals.

He has fond memories of his first Group One winner, Rebelline, in the Tattersalls Gold Cup at the Curragh in 2001. McDonagh speaks very highly of Lady Chryss O'Reilly, owner of Rebelline and a great supporter of his riding career.

As long as he is at the top of his game and getting the support of owners and his governor, Kevin Prendergast, McDonagh has no ambition to try his luck in the UK. More importantly, he wants a few more jockeys championships in Ireland under his belt.

McDonagh is sponsored by Norman Ormiston's Blackwater House Stud in Kells and, who has horses in training with Prendergast.

With the long days and even longer evenings during the summer months, McDonagh likes to just wind down in front of the television watching other sport.

Declan has no family of his own but has two older sisters, Shona and Ashling.

His father, Des, will always be remembered for his training of Monksfield, dual Champion Hurdler in the late 1970s while his mother, Helen, was an accomplished rider herself.

Declan McDonagh

Johnny Murtagh

Johnny Murtagh enrolled at the racing school in 1985 for a two week course and, was fortunately accepted to go on to do the full 10 month apprenticeship course. On completion, young Murtagh was sent to the stables of John Oxx for three months and, in the end had a long and happy association with the master of Currabeg which spanned 18 years, many classic winners and countless other group winners.

In that time, Murtagh was three-times champion jockey and rode such great horses as Sinndar, Alamshar, Ridgewood Pearl, Timarida, Key Change etc. As well as riding the first two aforementioned to victory in the Irish Derby, he has ridden three horses to victory in the Epsom Derby, Sinndar, High Chaparral and Motivator and, has been placed on four other occasions. In 1995, Murtagh accompanied Ridgewood Pearl to three of her four Group One victories in four different countries.

After the amicable separation with Oxx, Murtagh plied his trade in the UK, firstly having an uninspiring season with David Loder and then a very successful term with James Fanshawe, riding Soviet Song and Frizzante to five Group One victories. Another season over the water saw Murtagh riding more for Amanda Perrett and Michael Bell as well as Fanshawe.

It was soon becoming evident though that Johnny was feeling more homesick and when the opportunity arose for him to return to the Curragh to become first jockey to Michael Halford, he didn't need any persuading. And another very good young trainer, Ger Lyons, also has a call on Murtagh whenever he is free. The relationship between the three guys couldn't be better and to see Murtagh, enthusiastic and still riding as well as ever at 37, is a great sight for racegoers. Johnny Murtagh is undoubtedly one of the best flat jockeys that Ireland has ever produced.

Towards the end of 2005, he decided to try his luck over hurdles and, at Cheltenham in March of the following year, failed by a head on board Halford's Golden Cross in the Ladbrokes World Hurdle.

He keeps fit by running every day, playing golf and soccer and when time permits, it's feet up in front of the television and Sky Sports.

Murtagh is married to Orla and they have five children, Charles, Caroline, Lauren, Thomas and Grace.

JOHNNY MURTAGH

Conor O'Dwyer

Conor O'Dwyer first got introduced to ponies via his school friend, John Berry (now a trainer), who invited young Conor around to his house one day after school in Wexford, to ride his pony. From then on, the bug got stronger.

Mother was a nurse and father an accountant so, there was no horseracing blood within the O'Dwyer household. But eventually, his parents bought him a pony so Conor would now be going to all the shows and gymkhanas locally.

When he was 14 he went to the apprentice school in Kildare and later, he was sent to trainer Frank Oakes to serve his apprenticeship. It became evident that O'Dwyer was too heavy to be a flat jockey. National Hunt was to be O'Dwyer's future and Francis Flood the next trainer he'd be working for.

For the last decade he has been primarily riding for trainer, Arthur Moore.

O'Dwyer has ridden some excellent jumpers in his time, Strong Platinum, Grimes, Joe Mac, More Than A Stroll, Youlneverwalkalone and Native Upmanship, on whom he has ridden to victory on no less than eleven occasions.

He has won two Cheltenham Gold Cups aboard Imperial Call (1996) and War of Attrition (2006) and two Champion Hurdles with Hardy Eustace (2004 & 2005). In fact, it was only after the untimely death of jockey Kieran Kelly in August 2003 that Conor got the call to ride the Lar Byrne owned Hardy Eustace.

His future as a jockey may seem near to retirement but the training establishment in Naas is already up and running. This hugely popular gentleman of the saddle will surely be missed but, after riding more than 450 winners during his career, one hopes he has continued success in the training ranks.

O'Dwyer enjoys playing golf and going sea-fishing back home in Kilmore Quay.

He is married to Audrey and they have three children, Amanda, David and Charlie.

CONOR O'DWYER

Pat Smullen

Pat Smullen's introduction to horse racing came via his eldest brother's love of the sport. In fact he was only ten when his father would drive Sean, Pat's brother, to Joanna Morgan's stable to ride work etc. Immediately, Joanna spotted this small, skinny kid in the back of the car and, thought we could give this lad a trial. That's where it all started for young Smullen, his love and association with horses had begun.

Four years later, when he had left school, Smullen went to work for Tom Lacy and served his apprenticeship there before joining Dermot Weld in 1999.

After riding his first winner, for Lacy in 1993, he became champion apprentice in 1995 and 1996. In only his second season at Rosewell House, he was champion jockey and, also added the titles of 2001 and 2005 to his CV.

Since teaming up with Weld and Moyglare Stud, he has ridden winners in Canada, USA and England as well as his native Ireland. Grey Swallow's victory in the 2003 Irish Derby has been a highlight in his career, but his most treasured memories are winning four consecutive Irish St. Legers aboard Vinnie Roe from 2002.

Smullen has also won the English 2000 Guineas on Refuse To Bend (2003) and the Irish 1000 Guineas on Nightime (2006). He also had family success in 2006 when riding Kempes to victory in the Specsavers Ulster Derby for his wife and trainer, Frances.

From Rhode in Co.Offaly Pat now lives with his wife and two children Hannah and Paddy, close to the Curragh.

Smullen is happy to remain riding in Ireland for Mr.Weld and hopefully, to become champion jockey for many more years.

With a young family and riding commitments Smullen has very little time for hobbies but enjoys spending any spare time he has, working on his farm.

PAT SMULLEN

RUBY WALSH

Ruby Walsh, arguably Ireland's finest National Hunt rider of all time and, still only in his twenties, first took out an amateur's licence when he was just sixteen. Father Ted who was training then and still is, was a six-time Irish Champion Amateur Jockey and these days is probably as well known as a television racing pundit, So, it was in the blood that young Ruby would be a jockey and that Dad would be their to guide him.

But within a year Ruby was off to ride for Willie Mullins and nowadays he combines riding for Mullins and other Irish trainers with commuting to England to ride for champion trainer, Paul Nicholls.

His first Cheltenham Festival winner came as an amateur on board Alexander Banquet in the bumper in 1998. Since then he has ridden twelve more winners at the Festival but the two that stand out would be Azertyuiop in the Queen Mother Champion Chase and Kauto Star in the Gold Cup.

Walsh has been champion amateur twice, champion jockey four times and twice leading rider at the Festival. His superb tactical brain and quiet riding style belies the fact that he is immensely strong in a finish.

Papillon (2000) for his father and Hedgehunter (2005) were his two Aintree Grand National triumphs, Commanche Court (2000) and Numbersixvalverde (2005) were his two Irish Grand National winners and he has also won the Scottish and Welsh Grand Nationals aboard Take Control (2002) and Silver Birch (2004) respectively. Add to that tally three successive Kerry Nationals and, the fact that a short-head reverse prevented him from becoming the first jockey in history to ride the winner of four Grand Nationals in one season and, you can see why this young man is being heralded as possibly the greatest jump jockey in Ireland's history.

Ruby has a brother Ted, and two sisters, Jennifer, who is also his agent and Katie, a very talented amateur jockey in her own right.

RUBY WALSH

BOOKMAKERS - PRESENTERS

Justin Carthy

Justin Carthy's introduction to gambling came via his father, who was a bookmaker at Shelbourne Park greyhound stadium. He would learn how to clerk for his dad and one day, when he was just fifteen, he was invited to work at Leopardstown Christmas Festival for John Brown.

After leaving school, Carthy went to college to study accountancy but soon found out that the "racing game" was more lucrative and, that you didn't need a degree to take money.

His first association with his "boss", Dermot Desmond, was back in mid-nineties when he was asked if he knew anyone who'd take a bet on the US Masters. Of course, Carthy, as bold as brass said he would lay a bet. The bet incidently was two grand each way at 66's on Jose Maria Olazabal. The result :- Desmond 165k richer. How did young Carthy pay up ?
Whatever, "a great introduction and a chunk taken out of you at 23 years of age", is how Carthy describes it. And, from that day onwards he and Desmond have struck up a great working relationship.

Since forming Chronicle Bookmakers (in partnership with Desmond), the largest winning single they've laid was 700k - 200k on Hardy Eustace's second Champion Hurdle.

As well as Cheltenham, Carthy stands at thirteen other UK racecourses but admits to getting a great buzz out of the "majors", Galway and Cheltenham.

He openly admits to being a sports freak and he enjoys playing golf and
watching Celtic, home and away.

Carthy also has nine horses in training with Swan, Wachman and Lynam.

One horse he was associated with, High Society, he purchased for four grand and sold for 200 grand. Is that how DD got his money ? ? ?

Wife Rachel must have the patience of a saint.

JUSTIN CARTHY

Frank Finigan

Frank Finigan first observed bookmakers at Dundalk taking money but, giving very little in return (some things never change). He then thought "this is the life for me" and first stood as a bookie at Mullingar greyhounds in 1966. It was not long before horse racing punters came face to face with Finigan and, with his terms of betting "without the favourite and second favourite". Thirty five years on from that first day at his local racecourse, he now has a pitch on everyone of Ireland's racecourses.

Looking back over the years, the one result that hurt Finigan the most, was the 1988 Aintree Grand National with Rhyme N Reason and Brendan Powell coming home alone. There was no way in Finigan's eyes (or pocket) that this bay gelding would ever win the National. And listening to his description of the last fence jump and run-in almost makes one sympathise with the bookie.

Three years earlier though, at Leopardstown, Finigan had had the biggest pay-day of his career when Bob Back was beaten by the Lester Piggott ridden Commanche Run in the Champion Stakes.
What goes around comes around, Frank.

A complete sports enthusiast, he will sit in front of the television for hours and watch almost anything with a competitive edge to it or, something he can lay a bet on.

During his life Finigan has been a very keen and able cricketer but, much earlier in his college days, he enjoyed playing basketball almost as much..

A genial and colourful character, Frank is married to Margie and has two children, David and Barbara.

Frank Finigan

GEAROID MOYNIHAN

Racing is about horses and humans. We all know that. The elation of victory and the devastation of defeat. Each has to be treated with equal dignity and respect.

As a person primarily associated with jumping it is ironic that Moynihan's first racing memory was as a child crying when Nijinsky got beat in the 1970 Prix de l'Arc de Triomphe. The jumping bug kicked in when his late father took him to the Shillelagh Hunt point-to-point at Coolattin. One of his heroes of that period was Billy Connors, a whipper-in of renown.

The people who formed his equine interests are far too numerous to mention but 'The Special One' was Norman Deacon. He was of the old school and he purchased a horse for Moynihan at the Tinahely Show. His name was Coill and the vendor was Denis O'Brien. Now there's a man who could produce a good 'un. Ask anyone at Ballydoyle.

And so of course to the man who formed the early career of Aidan O'Brien - and half the racing world besides - JSB. After a ten year spell in the techno world, Moynihan's association with the racing world was prompted by a call to Jim, who didn't know him from Adam, dished out advice in his own inimitable manner. Now Moynihan gets great pleasure to be in the parade ring welcoming him or his family to the winner's circle.

Moynihan says "From Leopardstown in the summer to Thurles in the winter it is a pleasure to be there. It's either in your veins or it isn't."

He continues "The Mullins dynasty have held an iconic position during my career. They all merit mention but Maureen was the force behind the storm."

Speaking of special mothers, Gearoid was pretty fortunate in that department himself and his children also. The circle has turned and now Suzanne, Jessica and Mark are all regular race goers. Jessica is, in fact, something of a self-appointed junior racing ambassador and has helped out at Gowran and Leopardstown on kids intro days. Something that makes Moynihan very proud.

Her first racing experience was when her mother, against doctor's orders, got rather emotional when Klairon Davis won the Queen Mother Champion Chase. As her mother wept in front of the television the poor child must have wondered if she would ever escape the womb.
Yes, that's right, she wasn't even born yet.

There will always be winners and losers but one day we will cross the line in unison. A handicapper's dream. That's one for you, Kevin !!!

Remember, there is no such thing as the last race.

GEAROID MOYNIHAN

GARETH O'BRIEN

-Gareth O'Brien, a native of Malahide, Co.Dublin, is well known as the presenter of the "At The Races" TV channel in Ireland.

His father, who didn't waste much time getting young Gareth into horse racing, was a very good friend of trainer, Jim Dreaper who, had such brilliant steeplechasers as Carvill's Hill, Merry Gale and Harcon at his Kilsallaghan stables.

At the tender age of five, Gareth was taken by Dad to local racecourses at Navan and Laytown and, regularly visited the Dreaper stables.

After school and whilst studying for his arts degree, O'Brien took a part-time job at Paddy Power's, answering the phones and taking bets. From then on a career in horse racing was beckoning as he went on to work for both Irish Racing Services and SIS. Working for the latter he was based in London, commentating and reporting before joining the "At The Races" team in 2004. To be full-time commentator for the Sky Channel would be the pinnacle of O'Brien's career.

O'Brien's most memorable moment on the track was back in 1995 when the English-trained Jodami completed an historic third successive victory under Mark Dwyer, in the Hennessy Gold Cup at Leopardstown. Runner-up that day was a certain Merry Gale.

Hobbies include playing golf, watching GAA and flying over to Glasgow to see his beloved Celtic.

Sporting heroes include, inevitably Tiger Woods and the legendary Jock Stein.

GARETH O'BRIEN

Hector O'Heochagain

More commonly known by his middle name, Hector is a popular television presenter and racehorse owner.

Born in Navan, Co.Meath and christened Shane Hector O'Heochagain he attended St. Patrick's Classical School in the town.

After having his own travelogue programme on TG4, the Irish language TV station, he won over an army of fans with his informal, candid and irreverent style.

RTE soon discovered Hector and he was invited to host two programmes, Only Fools Buy Horses, which took a satirical view at the world of racehorse ownership, a sport in which likes to be involved with and Hanging With Hector, which featured Hector spending time with many different celebrities interviewing them in both Irish and English.

As well as his love of horse racing, he attends Navan and Bellewstown whenever his hectic schedule allows, Hector is an ardent Meath gaelic football fan and was a member of the winning 1996 All-Ireland football team.

He has a general wide interest in sport and music and his all-time hero is "whoever founded Navan, the greatest place on earth".

HECTOR O'HEOCHAGAIN

TRACY PIGGOTT

It was in 1986 that Tracy decided Ireland was to be her future home. When Tracy was a young girl her father, the legendary Lester Piggott, used to bring her to places like the Curragh whenever he had rides for Vincent O'Brien and, with her mother involved in sales, frequent trips to Goffs and Tattersalls were also on the agenda.

Her first job in Ireland was at a stud farm in Co.Wexford but with little experience of stud work and, being away from the hub of racing, it wasn't long before she moved up to the Curragh. It was on an invite from Tommy Stack that Tracy moved knowing that riding out on the gallops, going racing and stable work was more to her liking. She spent nearly three happy years with the Stacks.

In 1988 Tracy had her first ride in public, in a ladies race at Leopardstown for Kevin Prendergast and duly won by nine lengths to shouts from the stands of "come on Lester". But it was at times like this Tracy felt at home here with the support and the friendship of the Irish folk around her.

In fact, in the week prior, Tracy visited her mother Susan who was in hospital in England with very serious injuries from a fall off her own horse.

Shortly after her riding triumph came the opportunity to work for RTE and her first commentary was the 2,000 Guineas of 1989 when the hot favourite, Saratogan, was beaten. Later on, with more experienced gained within the media, Tracy was given her own Saturday afternoon sports show which lasted for five years. She followed that by having her own chat show and hosting quiz shows.

Tracy is now an owner of racehorses and with with partner, Steve Mahon, training them for her, life in the Emerald Isle just gets better. They are due to have their first child towards the end of 2007 and may we wish them continued happiness and success.

TRACY PIGGOTT

Paddy Power

The Power bookmaking dynasty dates back to 1894 when Paddy's great-grandfather, Richard, took a day off work to go racing, bumped into his boss at the races and was promptly told, "don't bother coming back to work tomorrow". Richard was soon shouting the odds at the course and when the first favourite was beaten, well..... the rest is history.

Now four generations later and more than 100 years on, the Power's are still operating on the rails. The Paddy Power chain began in the mid 1980's when John Corcoran, Stuart Kenny and David Power created an alliance to prevent a British monopoly and influx of bookmakers.

Young Power left college in 1995 at the age of 20 to work full-time within the industry, but during his time at the DCU he studied 'business studies' at degree level. It was not long after leaving college he worked primarily in the betting shops, marking the boards, odds compiling etc before finding his niche working with the media and managing public relations. He aimed to "sell the story and paint Ireland and England green".

Growth in the UK has now expanded to over 60 shops in London with 75% of online customers based within the UK. This appears to provide clues as to future betting proposals. The number of shops in Ireland is nearly treble that figure.

Whether the Paddy Power organisation would be here today was left to chance back in the nineties when, on St.Patrick's Day, PP offered to its punters a "double the odds" on any Irish winner. A horse from the Noel Meade stable, Heist, was a 9/4 favourite for a race at the Cheltenham Festival but, effectively 9/2 on the PP boards. Queues were forming at all of their shops hoping to relieve the company of a few quid. But, as is many a case, another horse came from out of the clouds to save them. It was a 16/1 shot, again from Ireland but pretty friendless in the market.

Away from the business, Paddy enjoys watching all sports especially the GAA, his loyalties are divided between Dublin and Waterford and also proclaims to being an ardent golfer.

Ambition in life is to see his colours carried to victory in the Galway Plate.

Paddy is married to Jayne and they have a young son, Patrick.

PADDY POWER